No Tear is Commonplace

Stanley Moss is an American poet, editor, publisher and art dealer. He is the founder of the literary imprint Sheep Meadow Press.

T0096347

Also available from Carcanet Press

Interviews and Encounters with Stanley Kunitz, edited by Stanley Moss

STANLEY MOSS

No Tear is Commonplace

CARCANET

Acknowledgements

Some of the poems in this book were previously published in *The American Poetry Review*, *The New Yorker*, *PN Review*, *Poem: International Literary Review*, *Poetry Review*, and *The Times Literary Supplement*.

First published in Great Britain in 2013 by
Carcanet Press Limited
Alliance House
Cross Street
Manchester M2 7AQ

www.carcanet.co.uk

A CIP catalogue record for this book is available from the British Library

ISBN 978 1 84777 250 3

The publisher acknowledges financial assistance from Arts Council England

Typeset by XL Publishing Services, Exmouth
Printed and bound in England by SRP Ltd, Exeter

The wilderness and the solitary place shall be glad for them;
and the desert shall rejoice, and blossom as the rose.

Isaiah 35:1

Dieu est seul être qui, pour régner,
n'ait même pas besoin d'exister.

Charles Baudelaire

To departed friends: human, canine, arboreal, avian

Contents

Sunrise – Morning

12 Noon

Sunset – Night

Sunrise – Morning

Paper Swallow

Francisco Goya y Lucientes,
I dedicate this paper swallow to you and fly it
from the balcony of San Antonio de la Florida
past the empty chapels of the four doctors of the church.
My praying hands are fish fins again,
one eye a lump of tar, the other hard blood,
my flapping lids sewed down to my cheekbones.
Time, the invisible snake, keeps its head
and fangs deep in the vagina of space.
Reason blinded me, banished me.
I fight the liar in me, selective desire,
my calling nightmares 'dreamless sleep'.
Blind, *coño*, I made a musical watch,
the image of Don Quixote points the hours,
Sancho the minute hand. I hear the right time
when I listen to my watch play church bells.
Mystery this, mystery that.
I have another watch – wolves howling and dogs barking.
Now the invisible snake swims in the Ebro.
I look out of my window to see time
as if it were not in my mouth
and all my other two-timing orifices.
Don Francisco, I swear at the feet of the dead who maim me
and the living who heal me that the least sound,
a page turning, whips me. I owe my blindness,
this paper swallow, to you, because I lived
most of my life, a *marrano*, in your deaf house.
I pull open one of my eyes like the jaws of a beast.

Nightingale

The nightingale never repeats its song,
sings 'I want to love you',
never 'Good morning, good morning'.
When it has mated
it plays hide-and-seek in song.
Some sing: 'My nation is alive'.
Whippoorwills and mockingbirds converse,
the nightingale pours out joy and sorrow.
When Mary was told a 'sword lily',
an iris, 'might pierce through her soul',
the nightingale was Atlas to the soul.
The nightingale does not tell lies in song,
it does not sing when it builds its nest,
when it protects its young. It has reason to weep,
sometimes flies south alone.
It seems it cannot be,
but sometimes it sings days and many nights
with its songs unanswered –
a gift to the gossiping forest.

★

The nightingale never repeats its song.
Does it compose
during the day to sing at night in trees
new song after new song,
write with wing and feather like the Chinese,
who paint the nightingale with a rose
calligraphy in the sky and song?
However the wind blows
for want of starlight clouds fall to their knees.
How long from is, to will be, to was – not long.
When stars disappear, the nightingale takes flight,
leaves us to birds that come at daylight,
that sing of love and heartache, and repeat their song.

★

Any bird can defeat me at song. The sky is a listener.
In Ireland, country of warblers and nightingales –
beautiful defeats. Canada, for ten summers, loons,
famous countertenors – hundreds, made me a listener.
In China, I lost to songs of joy, flocks
of green magpies overhead, omens of good fortune.
I hear everyday birds. I am ashamed I do not listen,
I go about my business, have nothing better to sing.
I am a ground feeder, a wild turkey,
sometimes a screeching Atlantic seagull
fighting with gulls over the guts of a bluefish.
I am not possible – half-male Harpy, a male Siren,
whose songs cause ladies to tie themselves to the mast
lest they throw themselves into the sea
because I sing how they and I will be remembered.
The universe is artless.
The sky is a listener, my mother now.
Call me Stanley. Give me a lake and a canoe
and I will sing the songs I've sung since I was a fledgling
confronted by the beauty of the wilderness.

Tell Me Pretty Maiden

No wrestling with an angel,
no dancing around, no to be or not to be.
The truth is I'm stuck with this constant
simultaneous remembering and forgetting,
each jealous of the other, each the other's fool.
That's the way it is to be alive,
tell the maple tree in October
in full foliage it is not constantly
remembering and forgetting.
Tell the ocean, tell sleep, tell his brother,
tell me pretty maiden,
are there any more at home like you?

I remember when I learned
female cypresses are wide in the hips,
males narrow, I looked outside my window.
A word here, a word there
and I saw the foreplay of trees
lasting from winter to spring
to summer to autumn – longer.
A maple stands by a maple or a red oak
a hundred years, two hundred years.
While remembering, forgetting myself,
a thousand adjectives fell from trees
in woods I know.

I try to learn the language of king maples,
more difficult than Chinese: hundreds of words
for green, yellow, golden, red, as Spanish has different
verbs to be for a permanent or temporary condition,
as Greek has the dual, a part of speech for twins and pairs.
The scrub oak has twenty verbs for the English verb to be:
to be tall, to be cut down, to be lonely,
to be covered in snow, to be a taker away
of sunlight and water from saplings.
I forgot I must go back to my life of
sums and minuses, family arithmetic.

I refuse to learn by rote, I forget
the greatest poem is the human nervous system.

I could play constant simultaneous forgetting
and remembering as tragedy, comedy or farce.
The curtain rises or falls on a simple set:
a nineteenth-century oak chair and table,
a transparent glass vase with water and forget-me-nots.
An actor says: 'three cheers for remembrance',
his brother Harpo brings in three chairs.
I remember the *niñas* in Goya's brothel
wearing two wicker chairs for hats,
naked except for chiffon blouses,
smiling at their leering clientele.

The years wander off like sheep.
They don't have a dog or a shepherd.
I'm old hat, back home,
constantly, simultaneously
remembering and forgetting.
Today while I rejoiced with bathers,
love stole my clothes and left me naked.

No Tear is Commonplace

No tear is commonplace.
The prophet said,
'Woman is the pupil of the eye.'
All beauty
comes from God,
butterflies
fly from and to God one by one
and to the forests of Michoacán
where Mexicans nearby make
Jesus Christ
from parrot feathers
and wings of hummingbirds.
You can hold such a God
against your cheek,
then you are as if
under a wing,
a firstling,
warm and comforted.

Why

I know my love of 'whys?' is a faithless sin.
I am a worm. You, Lord, are my Robin.
I think the Holy Spirit is a Crow, a Dove, any bird.
Born beyond redemption, I will never repent,
I curl around the serpent,
temptation to temptation, disobedient.
I never swallowed that You made the firmament, Your Word
that in the beginning was the Word.
I swallow my foolish questions – many 'whys?'
I pick from between my teeth the letter 'y'.
I am not wise. Now I am absurd.

Since there is no place in heaven for curiosity
or anyone with my beliefs,
I will take in the long haul earthly simplicity –
I will sleep with Mother Nature, my weak spot,
perhaps dreaming of questions, not in a Greek pot
but in the dirt among the leaves
parked under an apple tree to rot
in a place less pagan than hallowed ground,
never again to fool around in the company
of any living thing that fools around with me.

One day when I am far from useless,
You will throw me still wriggling in the river of loneliness
while You listen to the praise of gulls, frogs' applause.
'Why? Why? Why?' Your grand answer: 'Because.'
Old Fool, I have no desire for the afterlife.
I want to stay here with You, to hang around
with Your trees, Your animals and my wife.

What

My first dream came with a gift of *What?*
the infant's first wordless question.
I stand before you a sleepwalker
rubbing out, out the damned spots of yesteryear.
A saint or zadig invented the words:
'¿qué causa?' 'what?' so we might ask honest questions.
In a dream of curiosity, I ask – what,
how, who, which, where, why?
The dream of curiosity stages matters out of the question:
dramas about the living and the dead,
where each often plays the other. A little rouge,
a little powder, a change of wigs, who knows what's what?
Night changes to day, and day to night.
You think it's all sun and moon, not trickery?
True I hold the portfolio *chargé d'affaires* of my life,
but I am a corrupt official, easily bribed
by a tree into saying 'beauty is the answer'.
I sell visas to Anchorwhat and Paradise.

★

What is an atheist on the temple mount, and way of the cross.
What says 'Rome's Wolf is younger than Manhattan's Mastodon.'
Rivers of what, what, what, what,
run into the ocean, flood two thirds of the world,
'The poet is the instrument of language,
not the other way around.'
Flocks of where, how, which, who, why – fill the sky,
while over Latin American jungles voiceless *Stringbirds*
sound cello-like purple-feathered love calls with their wings –
now stringed instruments – a dark paradoxical gift,
like John Milton's gift of inner sight after his loss of outer sight.

★

There is no proof that reality simply is what is.
What – does not enter the past but is entered by it.

18

What – protects the truth by offering itself
as prey to the raptor *fact*.
The *Stringbird* is never caged,
as gods are caged in houses of worship.
Sometimes I hear its wings calling in the woods.
What…happens…is never quite comprehended.
What is a tree whose roots are a bear's heart;
the blood of *What* flows in mountain streams and rivers,
past gothic spines of ocean life.
Because Proverbs says,
'The leech has two daughters –
Give and Give!…and the fire never says enough' –
I remember Kunitz put in a garden for Cal Lowell
and Caroline, in Ireland. When Stanley returned
in June, he found only wildflowers in rubble.
Still, walking with them across their hillside,
hell and love glances in their eyes,
there was reason to hope because of love,
laughter and nightingales, the lovers might find
the golden bough that once allowed a Roman
to pass safely through the underworld –
but dreadful, unwanted guests were coming.
What's to do? Turn the key, it may unlock or lock the door.

★

Now death is in fashion but life's not out of style,
whatever the hemline, glove or cuff.
I don't see proof death's worthwhile.
It never says *enough*.
I spit in death's ocean.
Death is time away
from love. Life is a notion,
death's here to stay.
Life and death are hand and glove:
life's the hand, death's the glove.
What caresses my face with love
smacks it with an empty glove,
heavy as the ocean.

Parable of the Porcupine

The only animal that cries real tears,
my porcupine weeps in terror of Sancho, my good dog.
A crown of thorns crawls under the lilacs.
With her just-born swaddled in quills,
nursing her child, impossible piglet,
she scrawls in mud, in rodent Aramaic,
something like, 'Do not touch me.'
Touched by two mouths now and first needles,
bless you for hiding in your sepulcher of leaves
while Sancho, his mouth full of quills,
in faith and hope rests his painful head in my lap.

Capriccio

Better if I had said in song what I wanted
from a lady beneath her window or in a car
or when she passed twirling a parasol.
I saw Goya knew about suffering.
He etched a baby a woman held by its wrists
and ankles, its anus used as a bellows
to flame up the fire. I was Goya's child.

It was just after dark, someone
reproached me for lingering,
I smelled smoke, there was an air
of constant discourtesy. I smelled something
sour, like the dirty yellow smoke of a paper mill.
Roads were out. Two colossal figures like me,
Goya's boys, stood in the middle of a valley,
one with a club, the other swinging a rock on a rope.
In the distance, the crowd divided, moved
in opposite directions, dark figures on foot
speaking useless languages.
I heard a woman screaming, her hand
reached out was half the size of her body.
Under cement arches I saw a heap
of corpses, Jews with amazed faces;
some still alive raised their heads in protest.

I thought changing my shirt
for a clean one was the right thing to do.
I couldn't close open wounds
with flaming iron like an old soldier.
La Verbena of Seville is a burial party.
On a summer Sunday afternoon,
if the sky is a family, the clouds and I are
useless brothers. To find out what
access to the unknown I might have
I played a blind philosopher who had fifty-eight years,
led by a street-wise, seventeenth-century
Neapolitan kid. I told the boy who led me

by a fold of my cape, *I live like the dreamer*
who in sleep seems to act and speak
but waking has said and done nothing.
I live in total darkness
where the most ordinary things must be imagined
and the unknown becomes less extraordinary.

I said nothing that made anything better,
so I put what I wrote away,
not wanting to be barely entertaining.
I think I lived between always and never.
I wanted to forget that. I was like a dog,
chin on a rock, looking up at the sky.

History

Two grains of sand, the ocean coming in:
once an Irishman in his coffin
had to be wrapped from foot to chin
in English wool, not Irish linen.
I saw this notice: 'Some striped scars on his back,
runaway slave stole himself, calls himself Jack.'

At the foot of the cross, I throw dice.
Expelled from Eden I throw rice.

Sand

My scarred tongue has been everywhere
my finger has been and for longer.
My tongue is gentle, my heart's cousin.
I have no time for ornament
thinking why the wind does this or that.
The afternoon breakers roll ashore,
there is little left in the sand,
a shell where my face was.
I spit out more sand than truth.
I go to my garden. I save the day
with dirty hands. Rain, rain, rain,
I'm sure the rain means more to the garden
than to sand. Then I remember creatures that live
with their mouths wide open, their tongues in sand,
that we first made love in a bed of Atlantic sand.

To a Stranger

Señor, make me a stranger to myself.
I am ashamed of my over-familiarity
with myself. My lack of respect
for my privacy, my way of asking
'Who were you, who are you?
Why did you do or not do, think, feel
love, hate, deny, believe or disbelieve,
choose to eat or not eat this or that?'
I am tired of walking through my own shadow,
my hands feeding me, washing me, shaking as usual.
Doing lightens the burden of words.
Let me enter the forest of decaying nouns,
to spy on the morning glory that blooms one morning
and dies that afternoon, unless it has the luck
of a cloudy day when it lives 'til night.
May I go south to a Latin jungle
where the moonflower blooms,
is pollinated by night moths in moonlight –
until its petals fall at sunrise.
I do not want to know more than necessary
to find my hat and coat when leaving
a crowded restaurant.
Your will be done. Let me laugh or weep
because it is Tuesday or Wednesday
or the other way around.
Are there more Tuesdays than Wednesdays?
That is the question. Jocasta said, 'O, man of doom,
God grant that you will never find out who you are.'

Bright Day

Vivo sin vivir en mí,
y de tal manera espero,
que muero porque no muero.
Santa Theresa de Ávila

I call out this morning: Hello, hello.
I proclaim the bright day of the soul.
The sun is a good fellow
the Devil's my kind of guy. No deaths today I know.
I live because I live. I do not die
because I do not die.
In Tuscan sunlight Masaccio
painted his belief that St. Peter's shadow
cured a cripple, gave him back his sight.
My shadow is a useless asshole, a nether eyebrow.
I walk in morning sunlight,
where trees demonstrate against death.
There's danger, when I die my soul may rise in wrath.
I know the dark night of the soul
does not need God's Eye
as a beggar does not need a hand or a bowl.
In my garden, death questions every root, flowers reply.

That Morning

I got up a little after daybreak:
I saw a Luna Moth had fallen
between the window and a torn screen.
I lifted the window, the wings broke
on the floor, became green and silver powder.
My eyes followed green, as if all green
was a single web, past the Lombardy poplars
and the lilac hedge leading to the back road.

I can believe the world
might have been the color of hide or driftwood,
but there was – and is – the gift of green,
and a second gift we can perceive the green,
although we are often blind to miracles.
There was no resurrection of green and silver wings.
They became a blue stain on an oak floor.
I wish I had done something ordinary,
performed an unknown, unseen miracle,
raised the window the night before,
let the chill November air come in.

I cannot help remembering
e.e. cummings' wife said, hearing him
choking to death in the next room,
she thought she heard moths on the window screen
attracted to the nightlight in his study.
Reader, my head is not a gravestone.
It's just that a dead poet and a Luna Moth
alighted. Mr. Death, you're not a stone wall.
You're more like a chain-link fence
I can see through to the other side. There's the rub:
you are a democracy, the land of opportunity,
the Patria. Some say you are a picnic.
Are there any gate-crashers beside the barbecue?
I'm afraid every living and once-living thing
will be asked to leave again.
The first death is just playtime.

There is a DEAD END beyond darkness
where everyone and every thing tries to turn around.
Every thing that ever lived sounds its horn.
And you, Mr. Death, are just a traffic cop.

12 Noon

Chorus

Today I saw the proof in the dusty theater
of my Y chromosomes: 7,000 years
before King David my ancestors wore
his invisible star, G2a(P15).
Out of Ethiopia or Tanzania
they hunted and gathered their way north,
ice ages before what we now call years,
past Ephesus, the Black Sea, to Iberia.
Some lingered behind, found figs and grapes
they shared with larks and wolves.
My Betters, I am a child of your hungers.
Ancient, present, and future Silences,
I invite all of you to a fish soup dinner.
Call me a ship, a freighter and crew, adrift.
My joys and sorrows are battened down.
In my hold is the dry rot of things 'better left unsaid'.
Drifting? I am on my old course: I need
to wake up not knowing where I am.
Call it love of wilderness, Elijah, chance,
my North Star. Waves teach me winds.
I follow Aphrodite and Venus, those streetwalkers.
I read my slips of the tongue as if they are charts.
My rudder is for waving goodbye.
Pardon, Silences. What is this? Sooner or later
a message in a bottle thrown into the sea.
I am still at sea. God knows I love a storm.

The Man Tree

The man who walks through a field in December
wears a blue suit, but above his shoulders
where his head and neck should be,
an apple tree grows
stripped of its leaves by winter.
The suit he wears makes him seem human
but his branches reaching up and outward,
higher than any man, make him arboreal.
Tears flow from under his jacket
and out of his pockets, like a stream in a forest.
The man blooms in summer, bears fruit,
walks through a field of hay and wild flowers.
The man tree never says,
'*My* river, *My* waterfall.'
A mounting lark never calls, '*My*... *My*...'
Except when it sings
'Come be *My, My* Love.'
The hawk calls, 'I have *My, My* work to do,'
then when the work is done, it shrieks with the night owl,
'It's *mine*, it's *mine*'
– is why death was invented.
Under a man tree a mother sings for a time,
'My child, my child, my tree, my tree.'

The American Dream

Stuck in my suburban flesh and marrow,
the static news of mass murder, Blitz, burning ghettos...
At fifteen I made love in deep snow
in moonlight. I did not go all the way,
betraying myself, Claire McGill and poetry.
She was seventeen half naked used her tongue.
It would have been a miracle, my first time,
not hers. Is she alive, does she remember?
I raved about Lorca and Rimbaud.
It would not be long. I learned to kill before I learned to rhyme.

I limp into her chamber, a goat with old horns.
I think she will recognize my ghost, young
and able to make her laugh, among the coterie
of ghosts she did it with, while I cavorted
with Maria de las Nieves, Eros of the snow,
obeyed the commandment Djuna Barnes
gave me when I was 23, waving goodbye
with her walking stick, 'Follow the heart, follow the heart!'

My heart led me to illusion, but it didn't lie.
I was manned, boyed, womaned and girled.
I learned to trust trees, blind trees, lonely trees,
forests. I rely on their wisdom – as I will after I die.
Today a child asked me, 'How much love is in a kiss?'
I said: 'I don't know.' She said, 'The whole world.'

Revenge Comedy

Running out of time,
I can keep time with my foot,
with or without a shoe.
Truth is, time keeps me.
When I was seven, my mother gave me
a Mickey Mouse watch I hated.
I purposely overwound it.

China has one time zone.
When it is 5 am in Shanghai
and the sun is rising, it is 5 am in West China,
where it is the middle of the night.
My time differs from street to street,
from one side of the room to the other.

So much happened that is always.
So much never happened that is always,
centuries when truth was painted
as the daughter of time.
Hard to believe God pays attention
to what time it is anywhere.
Running out of time,
years, degrees, minutes are dirty little words.

When I was a child I slept as a child,
the sun used to wake me and my mother.
We had intimate conversations while my father slept.
He awoke and lived with nightmares in his eyes,
perplexed, enlightened, without a Guide –
son and assassin, a boy, I was his disciple.
He and I fished with copper line, a gut leader
and a spoon for landlocked salmon.
He caught one beauty. It was, he said,
the happiest moment of his life.
My father was whipped by time
and he whipped back. I was in the middle.

What was knifing him, cutting out the flesh
under his shell I never understood.

Now I wake at dawn, the sun mothers me.
My father sees to it and I say okay,
every day is a school day.
Until I was 50, I never wore a watch,
then like Antonio Machado, I set my watch back
24 hours. My sundial never tells lies
when the sun is down.

Letter to a Fish

I caught you and loved you when I was three
before I knew the word death –
it was a little like picking an apple off a tree.
At 20, I caught you, kissed you, and let you go.
You swam off like quicksilver.
The Greeks thought a little like that the world began.
You splashed and smacked your tail, made a rainbow.
Funny what drowns a man gives you breath.
Where are you, in ocean, brook, or river?
You suffer danger, but cannot weep as I can.
They say one God made the Holy books.
I offer Him my flies, spinners, feathered hooks –
not prayers. I swim with you in the great beneath,
to the headwaters of the unknown, in the hours
before dawn when fish and men exchange metaphors.

The Fish Answers

My school saw the Red Sea parted – you speak
to me only in North Sea everyday English
or Cape Cod American – why not ancient Greek?
I speak the languages of all those who fish
for me, and I speak Frog, Turtle, and Crocodile.
The waters are calm, come swim with me a while.
Look, the little fish will inherit the earth
and seas. Fish as you would have others fish for you!
Swallow the hook of happiness and mirth,
baited with poetry, the miraculous rescue.
I read drowned books. The Lord is many.
I heard this gossip in Long Island Sound:
Three days before he died, one Ezra Pound
told a friend, 'Go with God, if you can stand the company.'

December 8

May these words serve as a crescent moon:
in Barcelona 58 years ago today
I saw on the front page of *La Vanguardia*
beside the main altar of the cathedral
two polished cannon blessed by the Archbishop
in the name of Saint Barbara, patron
of Generalissimo Franco's artillery
on this day set aside to celebrate
the Immaculate Conception.

Today in a Greek gallery off 5th Avenue
I saw Aphrodite blinded by a Christian,
a cross chiseled into her eyes and forehead.
Outside in a hard rain, Christmas season,
no taxis. I was chased by the wind
through the open door of Saint Patrick's Cathedral.
Up since 4, I slept in the false Gothic darkness.
A bell announcing the Holy Spirit woke me
to a mass celebrating the Immaculate Conception.
Can a Jew by chance receive a little touch of absolution –
like a touch of a painter's brush
like a little touch of King Harry
visiting his troops in the night before Agincourt?
I have prayers put in my head
like paper prayers in the cracks of the wailing wall.
The heart has reason, reason does not know.

Please

Please may be a town in Oklahoma,
but in my GI track doctor's waiting room
an old man in a wheelchair
kept repeating the word please:
pleaseplease   please   please   please
without stop at intervals endlessly.
I thought his 'pleases' had different meanings:
Please,   please says 'help the pain is killing me!'
Then there were pleadings to have a shot,
one I thought a prayer, useless without praise.
Could he crash into paradise with one word?
I remember the cries of sailors screaming in pain
without words or legs or arms
the pain coming from limbs not there.
'Phantom.' *Please   please. Please.*
I think every living thing no matter how rude
has a way of asking   *please   please   please.*
Please is not like a telephone that keeps ringing.
At the American Hotel, 'Lady Lowell' cried, 'Please,
please kill me. Please, please kill me,'
while eating steak. I said no, she said why not?
I said, because tomorrow's Thursday.

Drinking Song

It makes no difference if friends and family
are ashes thrown into the ocean,
or flesh and bone buried in holy ground,
their names barely attached. Awake or dreaming,
I see them as they were young and old, living
some other life, never in rags, never dressed to kill.
I don't trivialize the dead,
put them in a playground on a see-saw
or climbing a maze.
I remember their voices like
warped 78-turns-a-minute records –
stumbling voices.
I drink 'to life!'
drinking a little from each glass 'to death!'
because everything that is has death in it.

Look, the dead are school teachers,
they remember our names,
they grade us by number or letter;
they teach, 'Fools, you don't know
how much more the half is than the whole.'
The dead are trees. We are cut from their lumber,
like paper, doors, frames for their self-portraits:
penciled drawings of ashes and fat worms –
and the dead are stars that no longer exist,
so far away their light is just reaching us.
Death is a doormat that says Welcome,
a good night's sleep, a handful of stones.
To a little death before I die! La petite mort!
Because the breast taken from the child
is a first death, I drink 'to a nursing mother!'
and a first death the Christ child must have suffered.
I do not sing of phantom paradise
but offer a little phantom pleasure,
justice delayed – a hacksaw
for the phantom pain Ahab felt
after his severed leg was replaced by whalebone.
A hundred years! Bottoms up!

Smiles

I argued with a dear friend, a psychiatrist
who didn't think dogs smile and dream.
I told him I thought butterflies, frogs and dogs dream
and smile — that the whole Bronx Zoo is like me,
but I don't think every Greyhound bus,
cheese, beggarman and thief is named Stanley.
I've seen trees smiling, dreaming, kissing and kissed.
I don't think the world is a mirror made by Jesus,
rather sooner or later, like Columbus,
every old sailor sees a mermaid, that Jesus
smiled and dreamed like us, and Judas
had a dog that smiled and dreamed like us.
My good dog Bozo ran wild with my shoes.
I smile because I sleep and dream old news
and secrets I keep from myself. I cheer my heartbeat
on while my dog smiles, mounts a wolf at my feet.

Granite

When I was five I loved climbing a granite boulder,
almost a mountain. I kissed it and grown-ups laughed.
Standing on top, almost naked,
I could see to the other side of the lake,
the lily-pads and forests. I felt immortal.
My father spent that summer
in Venice and Vienna.

I remember an August storm, I was in the clouds
surrounded by my thunder, lightning, and rain.
I loved that, but I lost my footing,
slipped down, tore the skin off my back.
I still have the scars and the granite dust
in the scars under my shirt.

Today I returned to the lake,
paddled along the shore. I had to trespass,
but I found my granite boulder.
I kissed her again.
Who else can I kiss that I kissed when I was five?
I kissed rough lips. I used my tongue.
I kissed the flowers in her mortal crevices.
Does she dream she is a dancer, alabaster?
I held my boulder close as I could.

Alexander Fu Musing

The truth is I don't know the days of the week.
I can't tell time.
I have lived a summer,
a fall, a winter, an April, a May,
which I say because words are put in my mouth
because you-know-who is trying to sell something.
My mother rocks me to sleep, singing
a Chinese lullaby about crickets playing.
It's not easy to know so little,
but I wake to wonder, I touch wonder,
I play with wonder.
I smile at wonder.
I cry when wonder is taken from me.

China Song

I did not say: *The peach blossoms are not as white
as plum blossoms.* I said: *They are beautiful, beautiful.*
The peach blossoms fell into a rage,
their faces redder and redder with accusation.
But I intended no harm, no offense.
There was no reason for anger.
Pity me on my birthday, the first day of summer,
when flowers have their ways completely beyond me.

Elegy for the Poet Reetika Vazirani and her Child

If life were just, for strangling her two-year-old child
before murdering herself, my dear friend
would be sentenced to life at hard labor:
fifty lines a day before she sleeps
in a bare room with a good library and her son's guitar.
When will she have a change of heart,
when will she take pity on those who love her,
when will the terror she caused her child no longer appear in the sky?
The sun and moon hang around absolutely without conscience.

On William Blake's Drawing, 'The Ghost of a Flea'

Blake drew a giant flea inhabited
by the soul of a man,
'bloodthirsty to access',
usually, 'providentially confined'
to the size and form of a flea.
This ghost flea is an inhuman giant,
its face and body part man's, part flea's,
drawn in pencil and gold leaf on mahogany,
tongue curled out of its mouth –
it clutches a bowl of blood
out of which it feeds.
On a heavy wooden plank,
near the feet of the giant ghost
is an almost invisible second flea,
a common flea. A dream of madness produces fleas.
Flea-bitten by wars and slavery, God's messengers
visited Blake every day, found if the poet prayed at all
he kneeled or stood in what he called
'the seven synagogues of Satan'.
Many days, the Angels of God brought and returned
the same message made human by Blake:
Every thing that lives is holy.
Afflicted, Blake rejoiced to see his dead brother
clapping his hands on his way to heaven,
while Jehovah held naked Jerusalem
in His arms, pressing her to Him,
holding her buttocks firmly in both hands.

A Glance at Turner

His last words, 'The Sun is God.'
He found truth in color,
the Book of Revelation useful.
He cried out against the four angels
to whom it was given to hurt the earth and sea.
He followed a guiding star, a flight to Egypt,
a donkey burdened with the Word
and the Christian nation.
He gave a damn,
more than the sun, moon or darkness cared.
With a palette knife and thumb prints,
he answered the question,
'If God is the sun, what is the sunset?'
– proof the most pious death is by a kiss?
On his palette, primary colors,
something like never-before words,
his dead father, his mother in a madhouse.
He picked cherries with Claude and Poussin,
knew Rembrandt sometimes painted with his own feces,
that beauty may stink to heaven.
His own suffering never washed out of his brushes,
his Last Judgment, an angel with a sword, standing in the sun.
He did not know Blake's *Last Judgment*,
almost black from working and reworking.
God breaketh not all men's hearts alike.
Blake saw God sitting at the window,
Turner tried to pour sorrow out the window.
In the distant sky, beyond the stars there is
no Venice, no Titian, the Sun of Death shines.

Requiem

i

His or her life was never as close to us as now.
At the non-denominational funeral home called Truths
they hold services in the toilet.
The corpse wrapped in sanitary paper
is readied to be flushed down a large commode.
There is a bathtub full of flowers, or a shower stall,
depending upon the means and wishes of the family.
The toilet lid may bear the name, the date,
written on disposable paper,
the writing in lipstick in a chosen shade –
'ravish me red', 'pink pout', 'muse'.
The flush turns the body around,
the head goes down first,
into the golden pipes, and then into the septic tank.
Should the body clog the pipes,
there is a hand rubber plunger.
No organ, no Bach; the sound of a Roto-Rooter,
a wire snake cleans up.
In the valley of the shadow, there's a toilet –
saints and sinners, we are all manure.
Sparrows peck at us.

In their houses of worship where truth sleeps,
priests, rabbis and mullahs dance for joy
because the soul is already in paradise,
while in icy Lhasa there are sky funerals,
bodies fed to vultures, the birds of the Gods.
Better to sing Holy, Holy, Holy,
wrap the body in a shroud, prayer shawl,
modest dress, or finery –
remember the ashes, perhaps still warm.
What is left of the dough around the Host
stamped out, not yet consecrated?
In Spain the leftovers are a treat given children
like a cookie to be eaten with chocolate.
Words hold the soul, a small bird
protected in the hands of a child,
thrown upward free to fly into 'what's next?'

Dogs

I built our house on Mecox Bay
out of an old barn and Greek columns,
a five-minute sail south to the North Atlantic.
In sand, along the bulkhead, I planted Montauk daisies,
red hibiscus above the sun-splashed waves.
My dogs played wolf. Swans nested, songbirds
and sea gulls lived their seemingly pagan lives.
Occasional osprey swooped in to earn a living.
All weather, times of day, seasons were welcome.
Sometimes coming out of the ocean like gods
three seasons visited in a single day.
I thought I would never sell the house,
the flowering trees I planted, the hydrangeas,
the day lilies with my dog Sancho beneath,
their blossoms something like his color.

Old, my mother and father were guests
at our bountiful table, surrounded by my dogs
Dulcie, Sancho and Horatio,
often fed from my hand and plate. Out of the blue
my mother asked, 'Will you ever forgive us
for giving away your dog?' I said, 'No'
and changed the subject.

I was taught from childhood to count my blessings:
at night when I called, my mother came,
good food, summers in Adirondack wilderness.
At seven I swam a mile across the lake and back
without a following boat. From an attic window
in Kew Gardens, above a maple, I read
with my dog Rhumba and pretended.
Still sometimes I went to school black and blue.
A kid of nine, I saw wonders of the ancient world:
there is a photo of me with the sphinx and a camel.
I walked along the harbor once straddled
by the fallen Colossus of Rhodes. A week later,
on the Acropolis, I was doomed and blessed
for life by Greek beauty.

I lived in a house of unnatural affection.
More than kin and more than kind,
my mother suffered from Metamorphosis:
changed from good wife, to pillow, to slave
rebuked for planting daisies along the driveway.
Still, she shared in taking down
her opinionated, overgrown thirteen-year-old
by giving away Rhumba, his old dog,
to a waitress whose face I remember.
I loved my dog for nine years. That mutt kissed
the eyes of my blind friend, came when I whistled,
gave seminars on love, intimacy and simple honesty.
Jesus said, 'Father forgive them
for they know not what they do.'
But Jesus never had a dog.

Thirty years later we sold our house
where I had entertained my mother and father,
buried their ashes in acid soil.
Farmer and gravedigger,
I transplanted two unmarked rocks,
Montauk daisies, my mother and father,
day lilies, my dogs, from garden to garden.
I recited prayers honoring my parents.
I only pardoned them. I never forgave them
for giving away my old dog,
despite my dog's teaching 'never hold a grudge'.
Of course, if my grandpas had not left
Lithuania for Philadelphia,
if we had not been free in America,
if I still managed to be born,
I would not have likely survived in Kaunas
to indulge myself in the fine distinction
between pardon and forgiveness.
I would most likely have had a roach
or a rooster for a pet, no dog –
my knowledge more Talmudic than canine.

Munich 2010

to Hans Magnus Enzensberger

I was pleased to see a one-hundred-year-old oak
and then lindens that survived the air raids.
Now the city seems to me lyrical, the smoke
of yesteryear blown God knows where.
Now sixty-five years are toast and marmalade,
are sweet and sour. The dead not here or there,
the living are here and there, have made the grade,
while grandma and grandpa fell down the hill
with another sixty million not Jack and Jill.
Thou shalt not kill is a bitter pill
to swallow. To be human is not human.
We must learn to choose the better part of human,
go back to kindergarten waking and sleeping.
Laughter is human, so is weeping.

For Georgie

Today, flying from Munich to Rome,
I saw Venice through Tiepolo clouds.
I knew Venus and Mars
were making love down there.
Two days ago, my dog died,
ate poison,
her insides were cut to pieces.
You Doges, Popes,
Admiral Jehovah,
Admiral Jesus, Zeus, Satan,
whoever is up to it,
I'll give you Venice, the Titians, Bellinis, Tiepolos,
the piazzas and palaces – *un affare.*
It's all yours. Give me back my dog.

Sunset – Night

Poem

Teacher of reading, of 'you will not' and 'you shall',
almighty Grammarian author of Genesis,
whether language holds three forms of the future
as Hebrew does or no future tense at all
like Chinese, may it perform a public service,
offer the protection of the Great Wall,
the hope and sorrow of the West Wall.
May language nurture,
be as life-giving as a bowl of rice.

Anatomy Lessons

i

At Piazza Santa Croce
I bought a print for less than the cost of a gelato,
an etching made when vivisection was a sin:
a battle in a vineyard: long-haired naked men
against long-haired naked men, Tuscans
cut open, dissected with sabers, crossbows and axes.
They do not fight half lusting for each other.
They do not take pleasure in their nakedness as bathers do
or fight for a cause, city or God,
or over a lover removed from the scene.
There is the artist's cause – to show flesh unresurrected,
how men look, stripped to bones and innards.

ii

With their book on love, *The Neck-Ring of the Dove*,
Muslims came to Florence from Córdoba,
dressed lords and ladies in gold and silver
brocades and taffetas – their poet-physicians taught
how naked bodies looked in life and death,
kissed and torn to pieces on earth, in hell and paradise.

iii

These days they pass a camera with ease
down the throat and out the anus, taking silent movies
of what was thought divine. Note: the sacred heart,
masked surgeons watch vital signs, seldom genuflect.
There is the poetry of sonar imaging, the heart, the kidneys,
the diseased prostate doomed to shipwreck
in the blood and urine of mothering seas.
X-rated and X-rayed, the body is sacred, love is still an art
some call 'praying': lying down, standing up, or on their knees,
whatever the place, the time of day or night they please,
when the body lets the soul do whatever it please.

February

to Arnold Cooper

A week ago my friend, a physician, phoned
to say he has lung cancer, 'not much time
so come on over'. I brought him some borscht
I cooked and about a tablespoon of good cheer.
We kissed goodbye as usual.
Then it was as if
we walked out in deep snow.
He was still in bedroom slippers.
March was a long way off, the snow
much too deep for crocuses to push through.
Then it was as if he laughed,
'I lost a slipper. Poor snow.'
I put his bare foot in my woolen hat.
We talked about February and books
as if it were a summer day. I thought,
'No better mirror than an old friend.'
He said, 'In my work I've done what I wanted to do.'
A branch broke off a sycamore, fell
into the snow for no reason.
The buildings of New York's skyline seemed empty
of human beings, gigantic glass and steel gravestones.

These words are obsolete.
We had an early summer. He died the ninth of June,
directed toward eternity like a swan in flight,
Katherine and Melissa at either wing.
Surrounded by love, he landed in his garden – ashes now.

Hibiscus, roses, day lilies: hold firm!

Listening to Water

Water wanted to live.
It went to the sun,
came back laughing.
Water wanted to live.
It went to a tree
struck by lightning.
It came back laughing.
It went to blood. It went to womb.
It washed the face of every living thing.
A touch of it came to death, a mold.
A touch of it was sexual, brought life to death.
It was Jubal, inventor of music,
the flute and the lyre.

'Listen to waters,' my teacher said,
'then play the slow movement
of Schubert's late *Sonata in A*,
it must sound like the first bird
that sang in the world.'

And there are African Links/Licks in Every Language

So if God made us in His image★
and likeness He's a black man.
Which did He hate more,
crucifixion or slavery?
Adam and Eve were black,
Cain and Abel black.
Somewhere there was
a white man in the woodpile.

Maybe God, come back,
had to drink at a Negro fountain –
wasn't what he meant by dividing the waters.
Black Jesus or Jehovah's voice
walked in the cool of the day.

Not that whites invented slavery,
they just made more money at it,
made it a Christian virtue,
found when they got a taste for it,
like good whiskey, watering it down a little
is better than nothing.

Do I see the Father come again,
sunning Himself,
passing the time of day
or night on street corners
out of a job?
If in the beginning was the Word,
we know the Word was African.

★ DNA evidence proves all human beings have an early black/African heritage.

Letter to Dannie Abse

Doctor, I could have asked but never did
why weren't you a teacher or a drunk?
I could have asked you about your caring for
the wounded Nazi Luftwaffe Offizier.
Poet, you wrote love poems in your old age.

Jew, not by chance your son's name is David –
honors the psalmist and Saint Davy.
We celebrate spring at the same table,
suffer the same wintry fever.
In a pub called The Good Life the landlord serves
with every glass of joy a tankard of sorrow.

Husband, I never asked about your marriage,
it would have been asking why there's morning
and evening. Welshman, we first met at Hay-on-Wye.
You said, 'The Welsh are a defeated people,
they identify with victims.'

I send you brotherly love.
You don't need a brother, but I do.

The Hudson River

A child of seven, I swam across the Hudson
at her source and rise in the Adirondacks,
at Lake Tear of the Clouds. I had her
where she is golden and sandy, ten yards wide,
as generations of swimmers have had her
in deep and shallow waters. I have spent many nights
beside worldly rivers. The Hudson is provincial,
sometimes like an overworked mother,
daughter, or servant. Her eyes and shoreline
show years of disappointment and disrespect.
Damn those who defame a sister of the moon.
She is indifferent to me – still, I have had her
it seems all my life. I fall asleep beside her.
Often I awake half-dreaming.
I see the Hudson is naked.
In the torn clouds I see a little boat with a light
on top of the mast. Is the light her navel or nipples?
I say that, but I know you can 'have' a mother,
not a river, not any other woman.
Swimming in the Hudson I learned I can love a woman,
'have' her, and she may believe I 'have' her too,
and that she can 'have' me for a greater or lesser price,
but we cannot keep anything but our word.
I bet my tongue on that.

Down River

to Zhou Ming

She remembered her dad's kissing-her-everywhere game,
her puppy pushed off the bed, not much about her old flame.
She could see his pointed eyebrows, heard, 'No rain,
no rainbow.' She remembered her Uncle James had a game
of pretending to throw his granddaughter out the window.
Why did she remember that, and what did that have to do
with the forced-upon-her pleasure and pain
of her dad's finger-inside-her game?
She banished herself for his smell and saliva on her pillow.
Smells can lie, but saliva's true as rain.
What she could not remember they would do again:
he is there, sure as hyacinths are blue.
She buried his ashes under a weeping willow
and went down river in a boat she could not row.

The Grammarian

I say, to be silly,
Death is a grammarian.
He needs the simple past,
the *passato remoto*, the *passé composé*,
the *le* in Chinese added
to any verb in the present
that makes it past.
In the pluperfect houses of worship
death hangs around,
is thought to be undone.
Sometimes he is welcome.
I thank him for the simple present
and his patience.

Affluent Reader

I borrowed a basket of grapes, I paid back in wine.
I borrowed a pail of milk, I paid my debt in Gorgonzola.
I borrowed my life, I tried to pay back in poetry:
an autumn breeze blew my poems away –
dry leaves, *insufficient funds*.
I'm still in debt for my life.
God is a lender, has a pawnshop,
hangs out the sun and moon, his sign.
He is in business 'round the clock:
I receive summons after summons
often in the middle of the night
demanding payment dollar for dollar,
for every year every minute and heartbeat
for every penny of my life – my death
plus interest: usurious eternity.

Space Poem

Universe after universe opens outward
as an ocean seen from shore,
where the waves and breakers do not roll toward shore.
They break outward toward
a region from which nothing, not even light, escapes.
I am there, beyond numbers and humdrum words,
billions of light-years away
with lightless, darkened, sun-filled,
begotten, misbegotten, dirtless stars
playing as puppies on planetary tits –
still not beyond what is. I think I heard
Emilia Bassano playing the virginal.
A caterpillar, I write riding a leaf in space.
I have only left or right.
I beg for east or west, north or south.
The maple leaf I ride blows out to a universe inferred
into and beyond amoral black holes
through its interaction with other matter,
unlike the moral silences between words.
The clouds I touch are as hot as the ovens of Auschwitz
and as cold as the gulags of Siberia,
temperatures I know from picture books.
I eat away on my leaf. I call from nowhere:
Sweetheart, have dinner. I won't be back in time.

Onlyness

to J.B.

Your Onlyness, your first commandment was:
'Forget about me. It's the passerby that matters.'
Was that my neighbor? I followed him into the crowd
but lost him. I barely saw his face.
My book of uncommon prayer commands:
'You shall love the stranger as yourself.'
Those without a spine with crooked hearts?
I saw a snake cut open, its heart exactly like mine.
He was a passerby. We did not walk the same,
but All-knowing Onlyness, You saw we danced alike.
I love the garter snake and the *fer-de-lance*,
but I cannot love my neighbors equally. At school I sang:
'Trust thou in Your Onlyness, He shall establish your heart.'

When years hunted as wolves in snow,
before the forests were poetry, the plowed fields fiction,
I was something like an Arctic lizard
that lived ten months a year under ice,
a dew of reptile-antifreeze in my skin.
You did that. Then one day You chose to make me human.
Your Onlyness, what did You ever do I knew the reason for?
What did I ever do I knew the reason for?
The rat holds her young tenderly as Our Lady,
sings a lullaby in a sewer pipe.
I am among the passersby.
I live with the music I love, that faceless beauty.
I think Your Holy Ghost is every living thing.

Eye

I owe much to my distant relative
the recently discovered
primordial ocean creature
an Eye surrounded
by a few transparent
gelatinous arms and wings.
The Eye prospered,
found food, avoided danger,
read shoals, corals, ocean bottom,
floated
out to sea, looking,
looking. Before there was hearing
or smell, an Eye swam,
saw. The evidence
is still insufficient
under sand, sunken mountains,
hidden perhaps in our salt tears.
Before primordial syntax
or love at first sight,
my ancestor, my ancestor saw!

Backstage

I am like a book fallen from your lap.
I can tell a tale of base and divine crevices,
of wordless places, unreachable ledges,
high waterfalls, clouds,
dropping down to swamplands.
I lingered on the footpaths in gardens
of lemon trees and oleander,
but my flesh was torn and I tore flesh.
Solo I dangled, whimpered, wept, begged.
I have fathered and mothered.
I offered fruit I would never eat.
I slipped into the furthest valley,
places without ornament.
I am Goliath,
a child has flung a stone into my head.
Actor in a dark theater,
I am *encoñado*. In repertory,
I forget who I am playing tonight.

For Uncle Lem

I have a Baroque painting – a martyr, Saint Simon,
is being sawed in half by two soldiers.
The saw cuts Simon down the middle,
does not bend around bone obstructions.
The painting troubled my uncle, a physician.
'Why glorify death?' he asked. 'Isn't there enough
death in the world?' I answered lamely,
'But it is a beautiful painting.'
I've been told – before I can remember
I cut my tongue mysteriously in two.
My uncle would not stitch it up.
He let my tongue dangle, bleed disgustingly.
He saved my speech.

Signifier

Ill-mannered, it might have been a death,
a sudden inhaling and exhaling, something before,
after, or during speech, not a word,
nothing to do with discourse, not a breath,
yet a blessing to a drowning man. A blessing
to the infant after the mother's breast.
I sing not of the wrath of Achilles
but of thin air and effect, a kind of aftertaste
that may be veiled, suppressed with a finger
to the lips, a sign of a certain changing, as water changes,
not tide, not pulse, not from the heart at all,
but a sign of life, a mumble within the body,
invisible, unintelligible, comic perhaps,
a poor, strutting player, signifying something,
unpersuasive, possessing tone, pitch, distantly
related to the yawn, the ah, without ecstasy,
no more important than this bass voice.

Silent Poem

I never took a vow of silence, but I am silent.
I walk thoughtlessly and thoughtfully through forests.
Sometimes I have nothing I want to say out loud.
I want my body alone to talk for me:
to touch, to hold, to love. My tongue can say a lot
without words. My hands have never prayed
or fingered holy tassels. My eyes, my ears, my nose
gossip about who I am, my nonsense.
A boy, some thought my noisy hair
would lead me to Delilah. I may be silent
out of ignorance, or a kind of cleanliness,
respecting things unnamed, the simple truth
without words, beginnings without words,
silences I hear, silences I keep secret.
I confess I shout in fury like a woman scorned.
I am for beautiful madness, fair play,
reversals in social status,
like Don Quixote dedicating his quest
to Dulcinea, a kitchen wench. I assuage
the ludicrous monsters of eternal life –
a three-legged priest.

The Carpenter

That boy who made the earth and stars had to learn
to make a chair in his earthly father's shop.
Above in the hip and valley of the rafters
held fast by joints his father cut
there is a haloed dove with outspread wings.
To the boy the workbench with its candle seemed
an altar, the tools offerings. That boy
could speak the languages of Babel. 'Bevel'
he learned refers to an angle not cut-square.
At first he heard angle as angel.
He heard 'take the *angel* directly from the work,
the only precaution being that
both stock and tongue be held tight to the work…
The boat builder bevel is most venerable.'
The person of the dove shook head and halo
from side to side, vented a white splash
that smelled of water lilies on the boy's cheek and shoulder.
Then a whispering Third Voice filled the workshop.
'It's time to make an Ark to hold the Torah.
Learn the try-square, hammers and nails, veneers.'
It was Friday afternoon, just before sunset.
The boy went to the steps of the synagogue.
He told the gathered doctors: 'God commanded Moses
Build the Tabernacle of acacia wood, gave
exact dimensions, in cubits and hand-breadths.'
The boy's mother called him:
'Carpenter, Yeshua, come to supper.'

At night the boy returned to the workshop.
He shoplifted himself from the Holy Books
and the forbidden Greeks. He grinned
at Heracles: a god deceived his wife, she threw
snakes in the crib of the misbegotten babe
who strangled them. The boy giggled at the great
deeds of Heracles and his labors, that he only
became immortal after being burned alive.
In the sawdust Yeshua smelled forests,
he could tell cedar from pine, from oak, eucalyptus.
He saw the valleys of death and life.

With his father's tools he cut dovetails,
male and female angles, lapped dovetails
that show on one face but are concealed
on the other with lap and lip, secret dovetails
where the joint is entirely hidden.
The boy had spent a sad afternoon with the people.
Why were so many ears, eyes, and hearts deaf to him?
He told them it was written in Chronicles:
'The house of the Lord is filled with a cloud…
the Lord said he would dwell in the dark cloud.'
The boy had never heard the word *kristianos*.
He saw his face in a pail of water, a cloudless sky.
He heard a cock crow, drunken Roman soldiers
laughing in the street. It was morning.

Squeezing the Lemon

If the table and chandelier
made for Wright's mile-high building
had 'social relations, hapless and unheard',
according to your lyrical experiment,
where might you go then to tell your story?
Where, *dove, où, ¿dónde?, nali* in sexual Chinese
nali nali also meaning 'you're welcome'? Nowhere.
A 'confessional poem'? Sooner waterboarding.
If there were a San Francisco earthquake,
would *Varieties of Religious Experience* fall off the shelf?
Did your mother speak for a year without a noun or verb
except in the last sentence? With barely a taste of self,
we are like prisoners in San Quentin,
salt and sugar taken off our tables,
two in a cell playing husband or wife on alternate weeks.
In a wink, you join with the one action that is death,
the broken nose of stars –
the last line of an unfinished style,
the last syllable of meaning squeezed out of a lemon.

Pollen

Still, near Santa Maria in Trastevere,
I saw a painting called *No War* and another, *I Love You*,
by an American woman eating a peach.
I was reborn in old Rome, still remain,
not a marble fragment, not a painting, more like
the Cloaca Maxima, an old, stinking survivor.
Much I had seen I did not recall:
ugliness and beauty, part of me
as music, unfinished work,
the wrong note effect,
– what I wanted to forget
and what I wished to remember,
that her lips upon my flesh
said, 'You are changing,'
then, 'You will never change.'

★

It is time to uncover the mirrors –
there is no death in the family.
It is time we wear each other's skin,
fur, scales, feathers, our mouths covered with pollen;
let's sing insect and reptilian songs.
It is time for the carnival of love.
I describe *caprichos*, I narrate beauty I fight for –
its protagonists and antagonists battle within the poem
down in the dirt. Beauty has a tale to tell:
ugliness and terror cut out of skin
and marble – a labor Phidias knew something about.

★

I can hear the earthworm's laughter.
Taught to respond to light, cut in half,
each new half responds to light – small stars.
It is time for asterisks, stars that point to human life.
May my liver, kidney and heart severed
recall good times – I was there
and I refuse to get out of here.
My head, severed from my body,
remembers love, perhaps irregular verbs.

★

What happened to pollen? We die without insects and birds.
My friend going blind thinks life is a dream.
I do not know why yet I live to say
I've gone to seed, I'm not sure of my name.
Winds carry pollen to quarreling cornfields,
on the same bush, a rose quarrels with a rose.
This dust produces that mud. I write in mud
with a stick, with my finger or my tooth.
I have found gardeners on their knees,
farm workers bent in the meat-eating sun
no less reverent than nuns. Every man's soul
is an immigrant, enters a new country
without speaking the language, works long hours,
attends night school. Reaching Paradise,
sometimes he longs for the old country, his body.

★

I go now, as a stone thrown out over a lake.
I should watch for the splash
that time between my hand and the water.
Imagine a stone flying:
there it is, up against the wild sky for a few moments
then it plunges down into the lake –
not the story of my life, but a typical afternoon.

★

In my ward of ninety-some 'casuals'
at St. Albans Naval Hospital
I wrote a love letter for a one-legged marine,
his good leg eaten by rats when he was in the sand under a Jeep.
His last name was Love. On his own,
he dictated the titles of popular songs.
A couple of days later, remaking his bed,
a nurse told me Love died, 'surgical shock'.
I was entangled, beaten by missing body parts.
Something of my body stays at sea, dismembered.

★

Virgil thought purple was the color of the soul.
Saint Jerome woke from a dream black and blue,
whipped at the judgment seat for reading Latin poets.
My body, bruised, turns purple, is hardly proof
my soul is at home in my body.
I walk knee-deep in a swamp, stinking of heaven.
A two-year-old child says, 'How disgusting!'
I am surprised the child knows the word.
Entangled in water lilies and devil's paintbrush,
I'm up to my knees in spirit.
Yes, yes, it pleases me to go into the dark.
These words are body. I try to find something
man made in the sun that is all over the place.

★

It's no time to die, almost everything's left undone.
Angel of Death, fly off with your black wings
with the first flock of starlings, with Canada geese,
out of place among swans with your thick, dirty neck!
I am what others abandoned
that I save. Rather than bury my old Bible,
I leave fragile pages to songbirds
that build, warm their nests and eggs with psalms.

Psalm

God of paper and writing, God of first and last drafts,
God of dislikes, God of everyday occasions –
He is not my servant, does not work for tips.
Under the dome of the Roman Pantheon,
God in three persons carries a cross on his back
as an aging centaur, hands bound behind his back, carries Eros.
Chinese God of examinations: bloodwork, biopsy,
urine analysis, grant me the grade of *fair* in the study of dark holes,
fair in anus, self-knowledge, and the leaves of the vagina
like the pages of a book in the vision of Ezekiel.
May I also open my mouth and read the book by eating it,
swallow its meaning. My Shepherd, let me continue to just pass
in the army of the living,
keep me from the ranks of the excellent dead.
It's true I worshipped Aphrodite
who has driven me off with her slipper
after my worst ways pleased her.
I make noise for the Lord.
My Shepherd, I want, I want, I want.

Index of Titles and First Lines